20TH CENTURY DRAWINGS · PART II

DRAWINGS OF THE MASTERS

20TH CENTURY DRAWINGS

PART II: 1940 to the Present

Text by Una E. Johnson

SHOREWOOD PUBLISHERS INC. NEW YORK, N. Y.

Copyright © 1964 by Shorewood Publishers Inc.

All rights reserved

Library of Congress Catalog Card Number 64-15862

Printed by Shorewood Press, Plainview, N.Y.

Contents

20TH CENTURY DRAWINGS
PART II

The mid-twentieth century artist as well as the scientist are both engaged in studying and formalizing ideas and concepts that often are invisible to the naked eye. In his search for a graphic equivalent to the visible model, the artist has turned to simplification of forms and speed of rendition in order to capture a calligraphic symbol and a spontaneity of movement as he ventures into the essences and wellsprings of an illusive inner reality. Where, earlier, Paul Klee charted a minute world within the discipline of his own penetrating vision, Mark Tobey and, later, Arshile Gorky and Jackson Pollock achieved through the magic of the "ever-opening line" a new conception of space and progression of forms. The artist is concerned not with a single focal point but with the unfolding of many layers of movement within a fluid language of images. Forms may explode or lie inert upon his paper. Thin lines may speed the movement; heavy, swelling lines may retard or abruptly close it. His drawing may be a deliberate exaggeration or an understatement. This pursuit of "psychic illuminations" has carried him into a total involvement with abstract imagery which has been designated as Abstract Expressionism, Tachisme, Drip, and Action Painting. The creative energy flowing from a rapidly-moving brush or a forced stream of color onto the carrying surface may be comparable to the complicated choreographic patterns of modern dance.

In this thoughtful discussion on "Drawing and the Hand," René Huyghe of the Académie Française observes:

> Of all the creative acts performed by the artist, the most directly legible is drawing. Drawing is also the first to which the artist resorts when he sketches the future form of what is still a mere feeling

within himself. Finally, it is the act that is most directly and spontaneously governed by his nervous and muscular system.

In a further consideration of movement and speed, he continues:

> Drawing is, thus, essentially movement, as much as it is the intensity of something dark on something light. The way in which a black is set off against a white, the modulation of the transitions from one to the other or the fixedness of the contrasts between them, all contribute to suggest a specific rate of speed. A spot in a drawing is as much regulated as is a sound. Save when these elements are deliberately neutralized, the drawing is nothing but an imprint—a secretion, as it were—of characteristics of life in movement. Like the copper wire that carries an electric charge, the drawing carries and communicates these characteristics. The pulsation of the drawing discloses the vital rhythm that gave birth to it, brings us into contact with it, and communicates itself to the viewer.[1]

In reviewing the great draughtsmanship of the past, one is confronted with drawings that have been sifted through centuries of changing styles, judgments and sobering hindsights. No such comfortable advantages are available in a consideration of contemporary works. Nevertheless, through changing points of view, drawings continue to paraphrase, in simplified terms, the expanding realities of the twentieth century. Their burgeoning vitality, their audacity or their tentative suggestions are apparent to an inquiring and receptive eye.

In the time of the Renaissance, a style was developed slowly over many years. Today, a single style burns itself out often before it is either understood or completely mastered. The modern artist must needs command a nearly inexhaustible vitality and tenaciously-held vision lest he find himself dallying with a passing fashion.

It should be remembered that throughout his life, Paul Cézanne sought to capture the basic elements or the underlying structure of his chosen motif.

1. Huyghe, René. *Art and the Spirit of Man.* New York, 1962, p. 29.

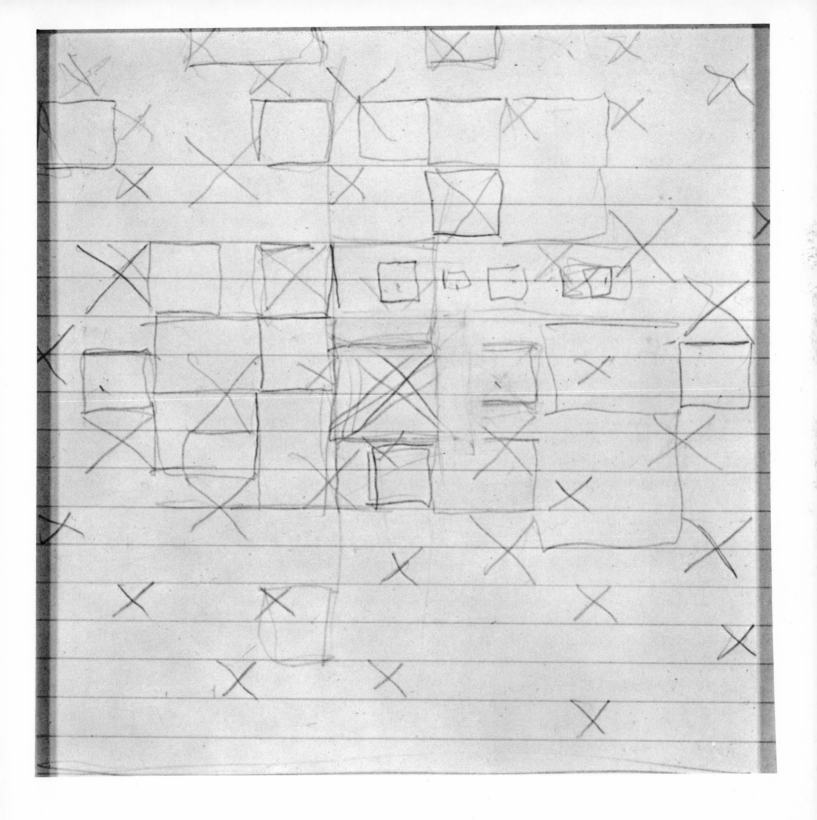

Pablo Picasso and Georges Braque and the later Cubists sought, through the breaking up and realignment of traditional forms, a new pictorial language, a way of looking at the world around them. Their continued efforts opened the way toward the further development of abstraction. Edvard Munch, the Norwegian artist whose work so greatly influenced German Expressionism, probed the shifting regions between dream and reality seeking to express the psychic realities lying beneath the visible forms of nature. Rouault mirrored an age through grotesque forms and slashing lines and forced it to consider his moral judgments. Wassily Kandinsky and Paul Klee, through the enlargement of their own artistic experience, sought a language of symbols entirely divorced from perspective and photographic reality. This was carried into Surrealist expression by Max Ernst, André Masson, Joan Miró, Yves Tanguy and others. Max Beckmann, through long years of exile, continued to reveal in traditional realistic forms his deep disillusionments and his own appraisal of man's disquieting destiny.

Authorities generally agree that out of this welter of earlier accomplishments the works of four artists became the major artistic influences that were dominant after World War II. These proved to be the expressionist paintings of Picasso and the works of three artists no longer living—Kandinsky, Klee and Mondrian. Perhaps a brief reference to their influence is in order. The section of Picasso's vast work that was of the most immediate interest to the younger generation of artists who resumed their own efforts after 1945 were his expressionist drawings and paintings which culminated in and followed his powerful painting, *Guernica*. The charting of its development through literally hundreds of studies, both in drawings and paintings, is a formidable but telling record of the creative forces which Picasso brought to bear on a ruthless destruction carried out in the small Spanish village. They also chronicle a receptive artist's dark visions of man's headlong pursuit of a demonic drama that seemingly leads only to his destruction. In discussing the visionary attitude of the artist, Rudolph Arnheim has observed:

Picasso did not deposit in *Guernica* what he thought about the world; rather did he endeavor to understand the world through the making of *Guernica*.[2]

As early as 1910, Kandinsky had renounced the traditional pictorial vision and had embarked on completely nonobjective forms in painting and graphic expression to convey his essential ideas. He declared:

> To each spiritual epoch corresponds a new spiritual content, which that epoch expresses by forms that are new, unexpected, surprising and in this way aggressive.[3]

Although detached from the main stream of modern art, the work of Paul Klee exerted a subtle influence on artists working in Paris and other European cities as well as in widely-separated areas of the United States. Klee had discarded conventional perspective and photographic illusion to penetrate to the very fountainhead of creative visions. Through his finely-wrought and disciplined lines and encircling forms he communicated his own experiences in an enchanted realm of dream and fantasy. In his pedagogic writings, Klee made the following observation:

> Our antipodes of yesterday, the impressionists, were perfectly right to live with the trailing vines and underbrush of everyday appearances. But our pounding heart drives us down, deep down to the primordial underground. What springs from this journey downward, whether it is called dream, idea, fancy, shall be taken seriously only if it ties in with the appropriate means to form a work of art. Then curiosities become realities, the realities of art, which make life a little wider than it ordinarily seems to be. For they not only put a certain amount of spirit into reproducing things seen, but make secret vision visible.[4]

In Paris after the war, Klee's teachings were reflected in the work of Hans Hartung, Roger Bissière, Wolfgang Schultze called Wols, Jean Dubuffet and through the continuing efforts of Joan Miró. Hartung and Wols fled to Paris

2. Arnheim, Rudolph. *Picasso's Guernica: The Genesis of a Painting*. Berkeley, 1962, p. 10.
3. Kandinsky, Wassily. *Concerning the Spiritual in Art*. Documents of Art. Director, Robert Motherwell. New York, 1947, p. 11.
4. Klee, Paul. *The Thinking Eye, The Notebooks of Paul Klee*. Jürg Spiller, (Ed.). New York, 1961, p. 93.

after years of precarious existence to continue their explorations of psychic and intuitive pictorial forms. Roger Bissière, in his later work, sought to express the essence of the intermediate world between nature and poetry. Dubuffet, in a jungle of lines and merging forms, combines naïveté and irony, compassion and cruelty. Perhaps, of the French artists, Dubuffet best understood the world of Paul Klee. In the United States the influence of Klee's probing and inquiring art was evident in the infinite nuances of Mark Tobey's drawings and paintings. In Germany it was seen in the works of Fritz Winter, E. W. Nay and Julius Bissier.

The "concrete" pictorial thinking of Piet Mondrian and Josef Albers, as reflected in their nonobjective paintings and sketches, exerted a belated influence on some of the young painters, architects and designers in Europe and America after World War II. Mondrian noted long ago that "the emotion of beauty is always obstructed by the appearance of 'the object;' therefore the object must be eliminated from the picture." He never regarded painting as an end in itself but rather as the latest development in the unfolding phenomenon of pure form. Mondrian was intent on probing "the realm of the pictorial means down to its primordial level—to erect the ultimate and most elementary paradigm of formal harmony at the very frontiers of the domain that lies 'beyond painting.'"[5] Today's geometric and "hard edge" composition in which there is left no semblance of the natural or individual elements, perhaps carry on with varied emphasis, Mondrian's and Albers' explorations into a subtle, visual language of pure lines, forms and strict color nuances.

In his creation of images completely devoid of literary allusion, Josef Albers has influenced younger artists in the United States where he has resided and taught since the closing of the Bauhaus in 1933. François Bucher has summed up Albers' life work of shaping new visual systems based on the supremacy of line and color. In his analysis of the results, Bucher observes:

> Albers' prismatic world full of visual spectra contains slight but infinite variations, each of which is significant and provides the emo-

5. Haftmann, Werner. *Paintings in the Twentieth Century.* New York, 1960, p. 203.

tion of discovering a hitherto unknown element. Thus in a sequence of visual events delight is created. Albers' ceaseless investigation contributes a new diagram of reality to the art of the present.[6]

Among the later exponents of "concrete art" are Victor de Vasarely, Jean Dewasne, Fritz Glarner and Ellsworth Kelly.

Not to be overlooked in post-war France were the older modern masters, Bonnard, Matisse, Braque, Léger and Ségonzac whose drawings of this later period maintain a sense of order and balance that is essentially French. Matisse, plagued by failing health, nonetheless was busily occupied with the project of his small white chapel on a hillside at Vence where he designed murals that were really large-scale drawings. A smaller drawing entitled *Dahlia and Pomegranate,* also completed in Vence in 1947, demonstrates the force and authority of a distinguished and venerable modern master. Possibly the expressionist qualities of his line and color appealed more than his intellectual sense of balance and order to the younger artists.

Braque, working within the confines of his quiet garden, filled sketchbooks and papers with graphic notations of plant and bird forms and flowing figures. With a practiced hand and a knowing eye he continued to record his abiding delight in intimate scenes and patterns of the world of nature. While Braque sought always to preserve the underlying beauty of the object in a humanized, lyrical expression, Fernand Léger chose symbols from the material life of his time. Details of mechanical forms and everyday objects have been the sources of his inspirations for his drawings and paintings. He once remarked:

> I have used the machine as others have used the nude or the still life . . . I was never interested in copying the machine. I invented images of the machine . . .[7]

He has also observed:

> Even a part of an object has its value. A whole new realism resides in the way one envisages an object or one of its parts.[8]

6. Bucher, François. *Josef Albers; Despite Straight Lines; An analysis of his graphic constructions.* New Haven and London, 1961, p. 75.
7. Kuh, Katherine. *Léger.* Urbana, 1953, p. 33.
8. *Ibid.* p. 40.

In the lucidity and charm of their late graphic works, Ségonzac and Bonnard consistently present a casual, personal style that carries forward an elegant French tradition into the mid-twentieth century.

The illustrations comprising this second volume of twentieth-century drawings begin with representative work completed during World War II and end with some of the avant-garde graphic delineations of the early 1960's. The art world of Paris looked with interest and with some apprehension on the first Salon d'Automne held in October, 1944, which was specifically designated as the Salon of the Liberation. Had the creative energies of the artist been lost or sacrificed in the long years of the war? Was a new reflective development possible? If so, what form would that development take? There were those who hoped for a return to a more classic tradition. There were others who understood that the artist would, as in periods of the past, continue the modern progression, whatever course it might take.

Many of the old modern masters were still active. Picasso had been given a special place in the Salon of the Liberation in recognition of his past achievements and the continuing importance of his work during the years of the Occupation. Matisse, Braque and Rouault worked on in semi-retirement. Léger, Chagall, Ernst and Masson returned from voluntary exile in the United States. Important too in the French scene were German artists, exiled before World War II, who came to Paris to continue their work after hostilities had ceased. Thus Hans Hartung and Wols pursued, as did Pierre Soulages, Jean Fautrier and others, the experimental direction of "psychic improvisation." The German artists came from a background that held the strong influence of Klee, Kandinsky and other members of the Bauhaus. Still other artists who had been active earlier in modern art developments in Europe remained in the United States and in England. Hans Hofmann, Max Beckmann and Tanguy lived in the United States; Oskar Kokoschka in England; Julius Bissier in Switzerland.

Figure 2

Rico LEBRUN • *Running Woman with Child*, 1948 • ink on paper, 18¾ x 25⅜ inches • Unversity of Nebraska, F.M. Hall Collection

Figure 3
Alberto GIACOMETTI · *Interior, 1951* · pencil on white wove
14 x 9⅞ inches · New York, J. Wilder Green

In Germany at the war's end, who of her once-large roster of twentieth-century artists remained to tell the story of Die Brücke, Der Blaue Reiter and the Bauhaus? Her vast cultural achievements and the rich holdings of twentieth-century paintings, sculpture, drawings and prints which had been so carefully gathered in her museums and private collections had been either systematically destroyed or sold by the Nazis long before the close of the war. Many of the masters of German Expressionism were either dead or had been forced into retirement. Still others had chosen to live in exile. Among the more familar names of the older artists who survived were Erich Heckel, Karl Hofer, Emil Nolde, Willi Baumeister and a few others. Oskar Schlemmer, who, with Baumeister, had hidden in a paint factory during the war, did not live to see the end of the conflict. Kandinsky had died in Paris; Ernst Ludwig Kirchner and Klee in Switzerland.

In 1949 Ludwig Grote, formerly of the Bauhaus, assembled, in Munich, a large exhibition of Der Blaue Reiter and of Bauhaus artists which brought a needed sense of continuity to the younger artists of Germany and belatedly made them aware of their own modern tradition. A few of the younger artists still survived who had scarcely begun their careers before the war. Fritz Winter, a former student of Klee returned from prison in Russia, E. W. Nay who had been a protégé of Edvard Munch returned from the war to continue his exploration of color values and symbols. Again, as had been noted in France, the exhibitions of painting held by Winter, Nay, Baumeister, Hans Hartung and other artists reflected the dominating force of Abstract Expressionism. K. R. H. Sonderborg's drawings and paintings in their thrust of color and swirling movement served as a bridge between the European abstract work and the American "Action Painting." To be mentioned also are the drawings of Pierre Soulages, Jean Bazaine, Maurice Estève and Jean Altan.

In England and in Italy before the war, non-representational works were generally unrecognized, and the influences of Klee and Kandinsky had been little felt. As they returned to their studios in 1945 and 1946, the artists began

Alberto Giacometti '51

21

to explore the somber and chaotic aspects of the disturbing realities of post-war life. To be mentioned are the works of Henry Moore, Graham Sutherland, Ben Nicolson, Francis Bacon and Reg Butler. During the years of the war, the English sculptor, Henry Moore, filled many sketchbooks with un-premeditated drawings which had no connection with a specific piece of sculpture. These are known as his Shelter drawings and were followed later by a series of Mine drawings. Moore remarked:

> I find drawing a useful outlet for ideas which there is not time enough to realize as sculpture. And I use drawing as a method of study and observation of natural forms (drawings from life, drawings of bones, shells, etc.). And I sometimes draw just for its own enjoyment.[9]

The painter, Graham Sutherland, has often made elaborate studies for his paintings. In the mid 1940's he began a series of drawings for a Crucifixion for the Church of St. Matthew in Northampton. Sutherland omments:

> About my thorn pictures—I had been thinking about the Crucifixion, I was about to attempt to subject, and my mind was pre-occupied by the idea of thorns. In the country I began to notice thorn bushes and the structure of thorns, which pierced the air in all directions, their points establishing the limits of aerial space. I made some drawings and in doing so a strange change took place. While preserving their normal life in space, the thorns rearranged themselves and became something else—a sort of paraphrase of the Crucifixion and the crucified head . . .[10]

The romantic elements of English art are reflected further in the drawings of Ben Nicolson, Francis Bacon and Reg Butler. While Bacon reveals a sudden horrendous vision of a secret despair, Nicolson interweaves intimate views of nature and abstract forms of immaculate clarity into a graphic statement that Herbert Read characterizes as being "obstinately English." Reg Butler, a sculptor, concerns himself with freeing the figure from its cocoon-

9. *Henry Moore, Sculpture and Drawings.* Introduction by Herbert Read. New York, 1944, Vol. I, p. xlii.
10. Arts Council of Great Britain. *An Exhibition of Paintings and Drawings by Graham Sutherland,* arranged by the Arts Council of Great Britain and The Tate Gallery from May to 9 August, 1953. London, 1953, unpaged [7].

like surroundings, or, in a more abstract idiom, placing spinning forms into undefined space. He has portrayed through his work the anonymity and loneliness of the individual.

The development in Italy centered around the presentation of human content in art. Perhaps Picasso's vision of reality guided such artists as Renato Birolli, Leonardo Cremonini, Giacomo Manzu, Marino Marini, and Ennio Morlotti. Other Italian artists came to understand that the expression of human meanings did not necessarily call for figurative representations. This abstract concept may be noted in the work of Afro, the later work of Birolli, Luca Crippa and Emilio Vedova, among others.

After the war, the work of the American Mark Tobey, who in the 1930's had spent some years in England, and the new work of Abstract Expressionism developed by the artists of the New York School were important factors in British painting.

The artists of the United States had benefited by the prolonged contact with the European artists who spent the war years in America. Masson, Ernst, Tanguy, Léger, Chagall and from time to time, Joan Miró. Perhaps the most significant influences were felt through the paintings and the teachings of of Hans Hofmann. He brought to many American artists first-hand knowledge of the problems and advancements of twentieth-century European art. His unflagging enthusiasm for painting itself and the steady development of his own style of large, free forms and brilliant colors caught the imagination of many artists.

The liveliness of the exhibitions in the New York art world also contributed to the excitement. Tobey first showed examples of his "white writing" at Peggy Guggenheim's Gallery in 1944 although he had been working in this vein since the mid 1930's.

In the same gallery in the previous year, Jackson Pollock held his first one-man show. With sensational speed he thereafter began delineation of a pictorial world of soaring and irrational chaos. Among Pollock's most monumental works are his large-scale drawings in black and white on paper or on canvas that imaginatively carry a new and sometimes terrifying drama of limitless, uncharted space.

Gorky explored many styles and his own ideas were often influenced for years by the work of Picasso. During the later years of his all-too-brief life, he evolved an eloquent and rich personal statement. Harold Rosenberg describes Gorky's approach:

> He observes the image that rises before him; he does not 'get into it' as into an arena. Psychologically Gorky's paintings (and drawings) constitute an investigation of the unknown rather than an immersion into its currents; their aim is in the conversion of the data through esthetic comprehension rather than an organization of the artist's energy as in de Kooning, Kline, Hofmann and Guston.[11]

It has been noted that the work of Gorky, Matta, Baziotes, Rothko, Gottlieb and Tomlin was meditative and sometimes tinged with Surrealist undertones. On the other hand, the drawings of Pollock, Robert Motherwell, Kline, de Kooning, Guston, Sam Francis and James Brooks charted the spontaneous expression of inner impulses. Although their diversity was great, they had independent vitality and conviction in common. First designated as the New York School, the forceful and strong abstract expression of their work made itself felt in the European art world and had considerable influence upon European artists. In New York the Peggy Guggenheim Gallery and the Betty Parsons Gallery pioneered in the presentation of the early avant-garde work of the New York group. The critics, Harold Rosenberg and Clement Greenberg, were among the first to perceive the developing elements in a new approach to modern paintings. A tentative summation of the New York School was made much later by the art historian Robert Goldwater in his *Reflections on the New York School:*

> He (the artist) is not merely a craftsman, neither is he merely a metaphysician; he is not simply a nature-lover (or interpreter) neither is

11. Rosenberg, Harold. *Arshile Gorky: The Man. The Time. The Idea.* New York, 1962, p. 188.

Figure 4

Asger JORN • Untitled Drawing, 1962 • ink, 5⁹⁄₁₆ x 5⅝ inches • New York, Mr. and Mrs. John Lefebre

he only an abstract composer. He is all these at once, and to categorize his work is to impoverish our vision of it. Except as technical device there is neither nature-into-abstraction, nor abstraction-into-nature; and where the device is not transcended there is hardly any art. Nor is there art, however abstract, which does not refer to visual as well as to emotional experience, though it need not recall specific objects. The artist has come to speak of the work's 'tension,' by which he means its vitality as an organism. That arises as much from its (however generalized) relation to an outside world of shared experience (a part of which is art itself), as it does from any purely internal construction. Herein lies the richness of the work. Out of it grows the coherence and the multiple individuality of the New York School.[12]

Today the artist has no limitations of subject matter and need not observe special taboos. Often he has cast aside the representational discoveries and conventions of the past although it had taken centuries to perfect the abilities to represent various facts of natural objects. Space also is freely organized to accommodate the individual needs of the artist or a particular visual problem. He interchanges background planes with the immediate foreground in his compositions to achieve an encompassing fluidity of movement. He has developed a visual vocabulary far beyond conventional or traditional appearances. He may not resort to direct observation nor even recognize the demands of logic. Perhaps in Abstract Expressionism the artist searches for a more direct and immediate contact with his era.

The preoccupation with Abstract Expressionism became, with many variations and repetitive echoes, an international style. However, artists of the New York School in the early 1950's took the lead in the exploration of new concepts and ideas through often unconventional means. In the total involvement necessary for the "action painter," a preliminary sketch or study merely slowed down or perhaps even destroyed the entire structural composition.

12. Goldwater, Robert. "Reflections on the New York School," *Quadrum*, Brussels, No. 8, 1960, p. 36.

Thus drawing and painting tended to merge into one expression which often became highly linear in feeling. A vitality of line was achieved through intricate curvings, knots, concentrated interweavings or heavy slashes. This merging of drawing and painting also is to be noted in the work of Hartung, Hofmann, Pollock, Soulages, Sonderborg and in the works of the Cobra group in Paris.

The name Cobra is derived from the initials of three of its members' native cities: Copenhagen, Brussels and Amsterdam. The artists who first worked together are Asgar Jorn of Copenhagen, Corneille of Brussels and Karel Appel of Amsterdam. Their basic idea was to achieve a direct, spontaneous expression through unpremeditated efforts. By this means they have set down on paper or canvas mysterious visions of strange animals, fetishes and amorphous figures and fantasies. Such apparitions had also appeared much earlier in the sixteenth-century paintings of Hieronymous Bosch and much later in the work of James Ensor (1860-1949). Although the twentieth-century works seem undisciplined and often confused, they nonetheless hold a continuing fascination.

It is not to be lightly forgotten that a large number of artists in Europe and America during the middle years of the twentieth century have worked within the general disciplines of traditional subjects and materials. They, too, explore and project through their chosen media "the inner world of man" viewed through the symbols and patterns of landscapes, figures and the myriad mundane objects that are part of today's visual experience. Among those artists who have penetrated into new, spatial imagery and various aspects of landscape are Nicolas de Staël, Alberto Giacometti and Vieira da Silva and Renzo Vespignani in Europe. In the United States, to be noted are the drawings of Kenneth Callahan, Gabor Peterdi, John Hultberg, Karl Schrag and Gregory Masurovsky (now living in Paris). In figurative examples, the strong drawings of Max Beckmann, Henry Moore, and also Giacometti give effective continuity to this group. Other drawings to be mentioned are those of

Graham Sutherland, Francis Bacon, Leonard Baskin, Ezio Martinelli, Jack Levine, and those of a very young artist, Michael Mazur. Lyricism and a shimmering mystic quality characterize the work of the older modern master Giorgio Morandi and the drawings of Morris Graves and Walter Murch.

Since ancient times, artist and artisan have been preoccupied with the combination of writing and pictorial images. The Cubists and the artists of the Bauhaus often built compositions around letters, words, fragmentations of words or specific names. Paul Klee perhaps explored every zone of encounter between writing and drawing. Charles Demuth in a related Cubist expression employed letters, numbers and broken words in many of his compositions of the early 1920's. Another American artist, Stuart Davis, made writing an enlivening leitmotiv throughout his mature work. The use of isolated letters appears in paintings and drawings of René Magritte, Jean (Hans) Arp, Miró, Bissier, Guerna Giuseppe Capogrossi, Simon Hantai, Henry Michaux, Dubuffet, Motherwell and Victor Vasarely. The elegant "white writing" of Mark Tobey and calligraphic forms of Bradley Tomlin give to their variously different compositions unusual spatial stability. This basic sense of the letter and its calligraphic value may be traced in the work of Georges Mathieu, Walasse Ting, and still later in drawings and paintings of Larry Rivers, Jasper Johns and Robert Rauschenberg. Much has been written about Oriental influences on the structural forms of Western twentieth-century art, especially those of a so-called calligraphic nature. Perhaps André Masson has pointed out most clearly the differences:

> ...the essential for the Zen painter means a manner of being in the deepest sense and not, as for us a manner of doing. For them it means fusion in the life of the cosmos, and for us a way of summing up.[13]

Drawings are the results of the artist's efforts to organize a vision, whether it is visible or invisible to the naked eye, into a structural whole. This requires the ability to select and to emphasize certain elements of this vision and to eliminate inconsequential details. On occasion, modern drawings have as-

13. Masson, André. "Painting of the Essential," *Quadrum,* Brussels, No. 1, 1956, p. 36.

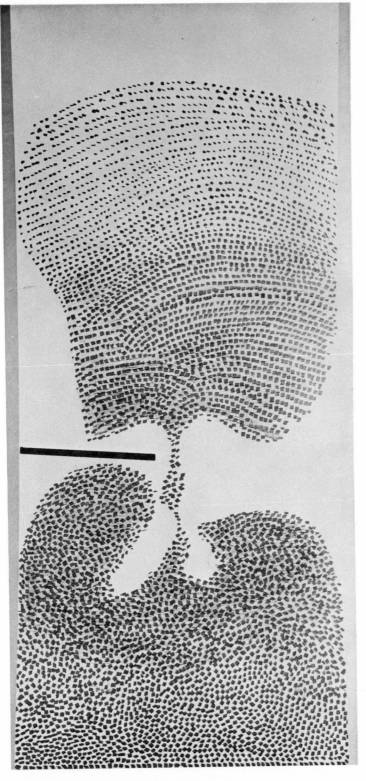

Figure 5
Victor PASMORE
Blue Development No. 6, 1964
ink on plastic, 48 x 24 inches
London, Marlborough Fine Art Limited

sumed the size of paintings. However, they are less involved with the heady slip stream of color and the heightened bravura of painting. They retain, generally, a certain intimacy of revelation and remain in Henri Focillon's fine phrase "a diary of human hand." The avant-garde drawings of today's artists are often harshly provocative, sometimes audacious and mockingly aggressive in what, on occasion, becomes a visually recorded fury of force. In their diverse range of styles and points of view, and, whether they are conceived as occasional sketches, studies for other more formal works, or complete within themselves, modern drawings often carry a mood of pervasive romanticism. This sense of romanticism and the creative excitement engendered by the intangible mysteries of discovery are acknowledged by the distinguished physicist and philosopher, J. Robert Oppenheimer. In a series of collected lectures he observes:

> Both the man of science and the man of art live at the edge of mystery, surrounded by it, both always, as the measure of their creation, have to do with the harmonization of what is new with what is familiar, with the balance between novelty and synthesis, with the struggle to make partial order in total chaos.[14]

UNA E. JOHNSON

14. Oppenheimer, J. Robert. *The Open Mind*. New York, 1955, p. 145.

Plates

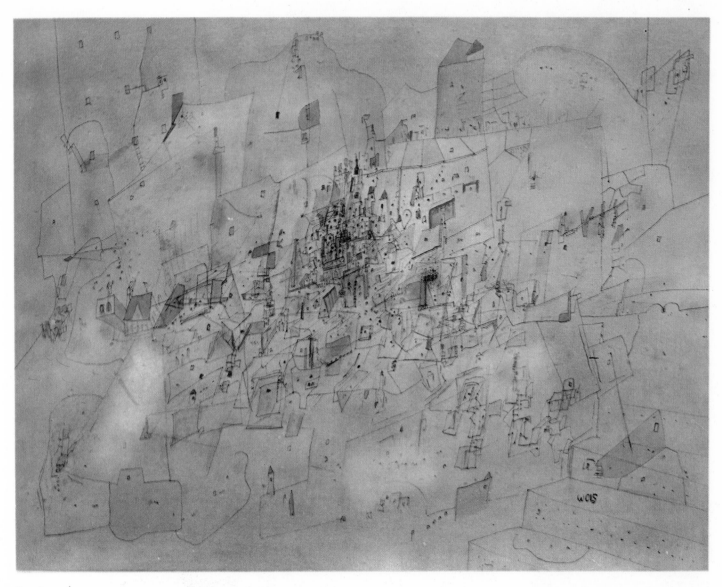

Plate 1
WOLS (Alfred Otto Wolfgang Schultze) · *The City*, early 1940's · pen and water color on white paper, 10½ x 13 inches
New York, Mr. and Mrs. Warren Brandt

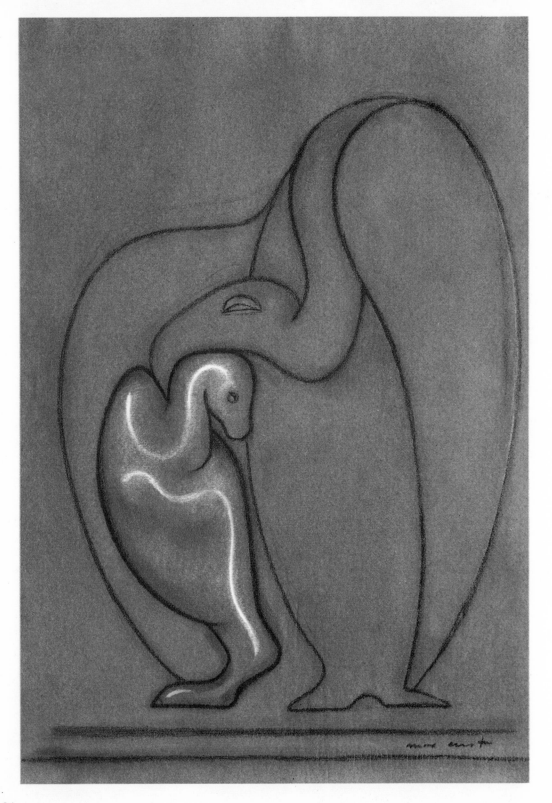

Plate 2
Max ERNST
Study for "Surrealism and Painting,"
1942
pencil heightened with white chalk
on orange paper
18⅞ x 12⅛ inches
New York, Mr. William S. Lieberman

Plate 3
Marino MARINI
Horse and Rider
pen and ink
15 x 11 inches
Pomfret Center, Connecticut
Private Collection

Plate 4
John PIPER • *Portland*, 1954 • gouache and ink, 14 x 19 inches • New York, Joseph H. Hirshhorn Collection

Plate 5
WOLS (Alfred Otto Wolfgang Schultze)
Sailboats and Elephant, 1940
gouache
14⅜ x 11 inches
Great Neck, Mrs. Heinz Schultz

Plate 6
Karl SCHRAG · *Rocks in the Sea*, 1963 · brush and India ink, 25⅞ x 39⅝ inches · New York, Kraushaar Galleries

Plate 7
André MASSON
Bison au Bord d'un Gouffre, 1944
ink
31½ x 23 inches
New York, Joseph H. Hirshhorn Collection

Plate 9
Alfred KUBIN · *Vacation-Time*, 1952 · pen and water color, 20 x 13¾ inches · Brussels, Mr. and Mrs. Stephen Adler

Plate 8
Max BECKMANN
Lady with Fur, 1945
water color
9½ x 12¼ inches
Great Neck, Mrs. Heinz Schultz

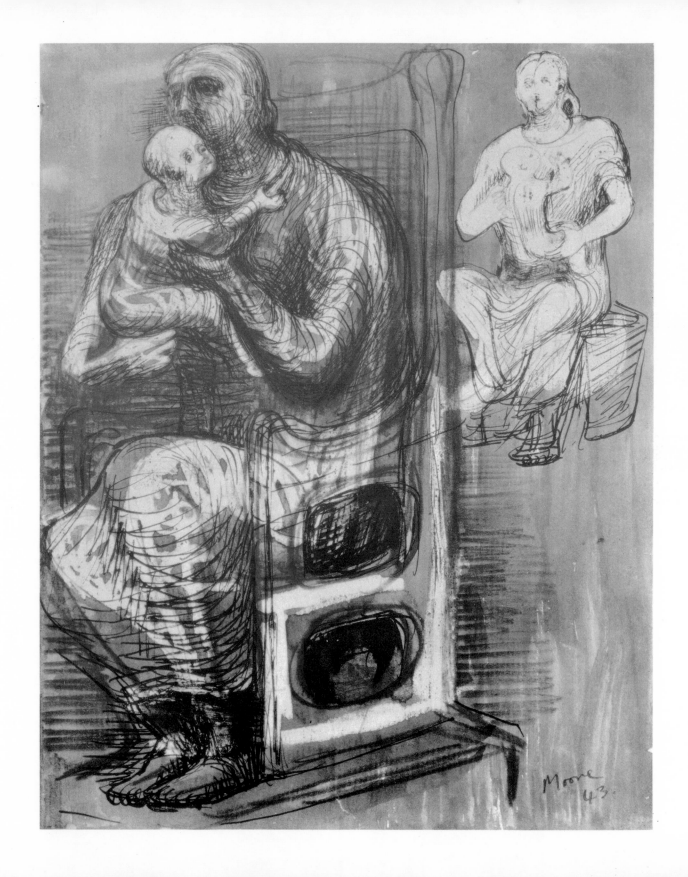

Plate 10
Henry MOORE
Madonna and Child
crayon resist with pencil,
pen and India ink, and
India ink wash on white paper
8⅞ x 6⅞ inches
Cleveland
The Cleveland Museum of Art

Plate 11
Jacques VILLON
Racine, 1945
(for a portrait in *Cantique Spirituel)*
pen and ink
11½ x 8¼ inches
New York, Lucien Goldschmidt

Plate 12
George GROSZ
The Painter of the Hole, 1947
water color
23 x 17¼ inches
New York, Collection of the
Whitney Museum of
American Art

Plate 13
Graham SUTHERLAND
Study for Objects, 1950
crayon and pencil
10½ x 14 inches
Great Neck
Dr. Gisele Fleischman

Plate 14
Pablo PICASSO • *The Picador* • brush and ink, 19½ x 25½ inches • Munich, Germany, Mr. and Mrs. Walter Bareiss

Plate 15
Philip GUSTON • *Ink Drawings*, 1952 • ink, 18⅝ x 23⅝ inches • New York, Collection of the Whitney Museum of American Art,
Gift of the Friends of the Whitney Museum of American Art

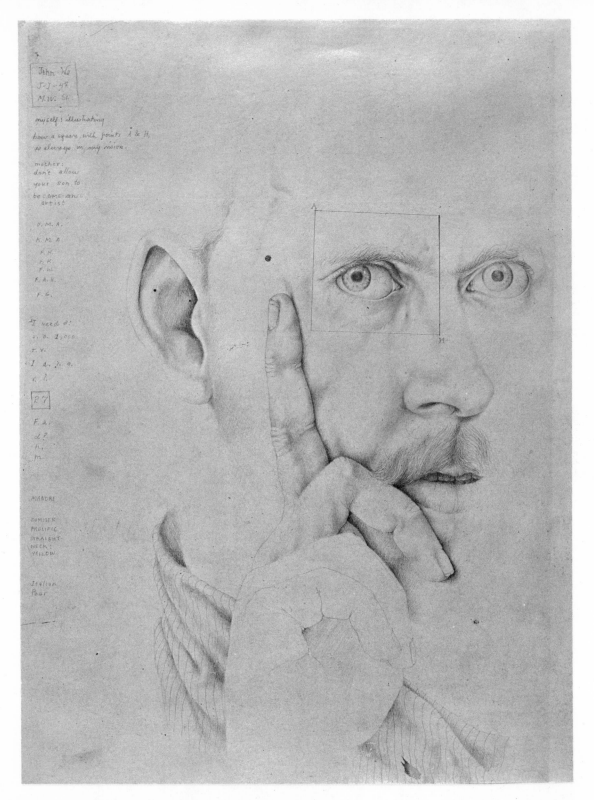

49

Plate 18

Yasuo KUNIYOSHI • *Juggler*, 1952 • ink, 22 x 28 inches • New York, Collection of the Whitney Museum of American Art

Plate 19
Morris GRAVES
Bird, 1957
sumi ink on off-white paper
34 x 22¾ inches
New York
Mr. and Mrs. John D. Rockefeller, 3rd.

51

Plate 20
Giacomo MANZU • *Artist and Model* • gouache, 19½ x 24½ inches • New York, Joseph H. Hirshhorn Collection

Plate 21
Andrew WYETH · *Mrs. Kuerner*, 1957 · water color, 21½ x 14⅞ inches · New York, Joseph H. Hirshhorn Collection

Plate 22

Yves TANGUY · *Drawing, 1952* · pen and ink with gouache, 21½ x 28 inches · Avon, Conn., Mr. and Mrs. H. Sage Goodwin

Plate 23

Ferdinand LEGER · *Untitled Drawing*, c. 1940 · pencil, 7¾ x 10¼ inches · Great Neck, Dr. Gisele Fleischman

Plate 25
Alexander CALDER · *Reef Fringe*, 1953 · gouache, 29 x 42½ inches · New York, Joseph H. Hirshhorn Collection

Plate 24
Hans HOFMANN
Untitled Drawing, 1948
gouache on buff paper
25½ x 21½ inches
Mr. Clement Greenberg

Plate 26

David SMITH • *Untitled, II*, 1961 • India ink, egg yolk, water color, 25½ x 39¾ inches
New York, Collection of the Whitney Museum of American Art, Gift of Candida Smith

Plate 27
K.R.H. SONDERBORG
Untitled Drawing, 1964
ink
30¾ x 22½ inches
New York
Mr. and Mrs. John Lefebre

Plate 28

Willem de KOONING · *Two Nudes* · pastel on paper, 22 x 23½ inches · Munich, Germany, Mr. and Mrs. Walter Bareiss

Plate 29
Walasse TING • *Untitled Drawing, 1963* • pastel, 11¾ x 14 inches • New York, Lefebre Gallery

Plate 30

Roberto Sebastian MATTA Echaurren • Untitled Drawing • ink, 14 x 20 inches • New York, Mr. and Mrs. John Lefebre

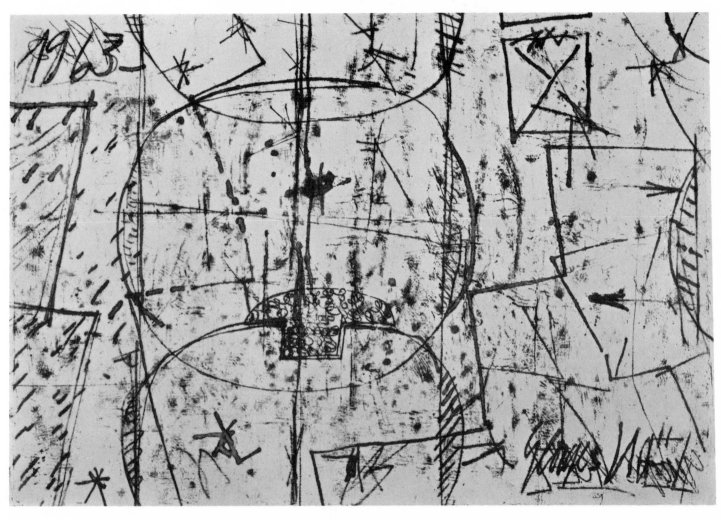

Plate 31

NOEL · *Manuscript Palimpsest*, 1963 · ink, 30⅝ x 21⅝ inches · New York, Lefebre Gallery

64

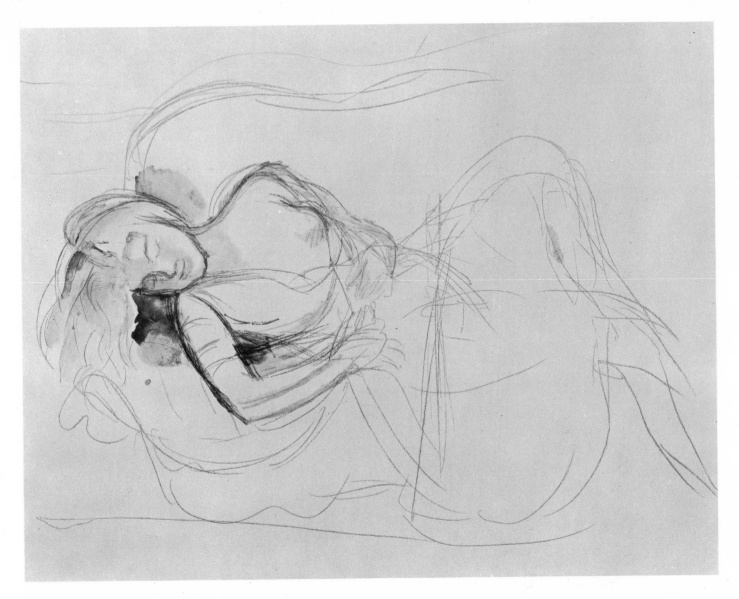

Plate 33
BALTHUS Klossowski de Rola · *Sleeping Woman*, ca. 1955 · pencil, conté crayon and water color, 17⅛ x 21½ inches
Chicago, The Art Institute of Chicago

Plate 32
Larry RIVERS
Self Portrait, 1953
pastel
27¾ x 20½ inches
Pasadena, Mr. and Mrs. Robert A. Rowan

Plate 34
Nicolas de STAEL
Untitled Drawing, 1944
ink wash
17½ x 10¾ inches (sight)
New York, Mr. and Mrs. John Lefebre

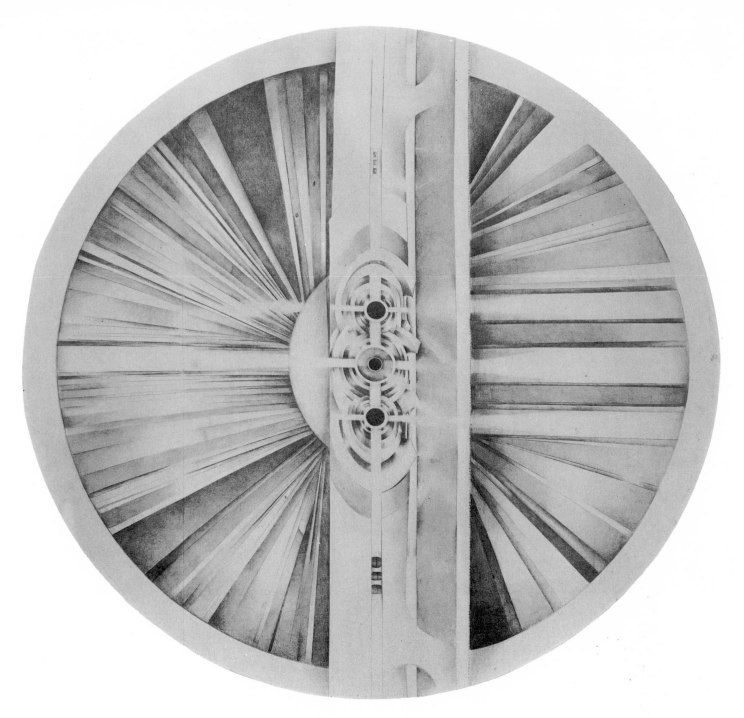

Plate 35
Lee BONTECOU • *Untitled*, 1963 • pencil and soot on muslin, 47¼ diam.
New York, Collection of the Whitney Museum of American Art, Gift of the
Friends of the Whitney Museum of American Art

Plate 36
Robert MOTHERWELL • *Kafka's Big Room*, 1944 • drawing and water color, 22½ x 28 inches • Great Neck, Mrs. Heinz Schultz

Plate 37
Julius Heinrich BISSIER • *28, January, 1961*, 1961 • oil tempera, 7$\frac{13}{16}$ x 9$\frac{7}{8}$ inches (sight) • New York, Lefebre Gallery

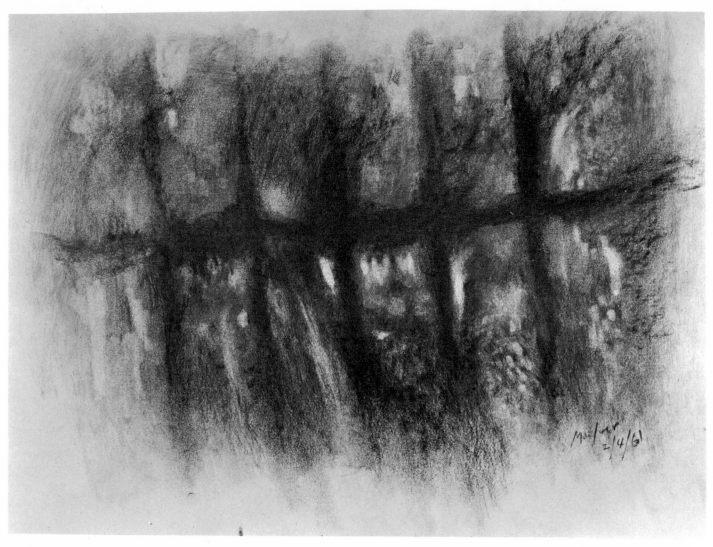

Plate 38
Loren MACIVER · *Blizzard*, 1961 · charcoal, 18¾ x 24¾ inches · New York, Mr. John Gordon

Plate 39
Karl APPEL
Paris series, No. 5
ink and wash on paper
25⅝ x 19⅝ inches
Worcester, Mass., Worcester Art Museum

70

71

Plate 40
Jackson POLLOCK · *Untitled*, 1947 · ink and crayon on white paper, 25 x 30 inches · New York, Dr. Jules W. Leaf

Plate 41
Cornelis van Beverloo CORNEILLE • *Speed*, 1955 • gouache, 6¹³⁄₁₆ x 12¾ inches (sight) • New York, Lefebre Gallery

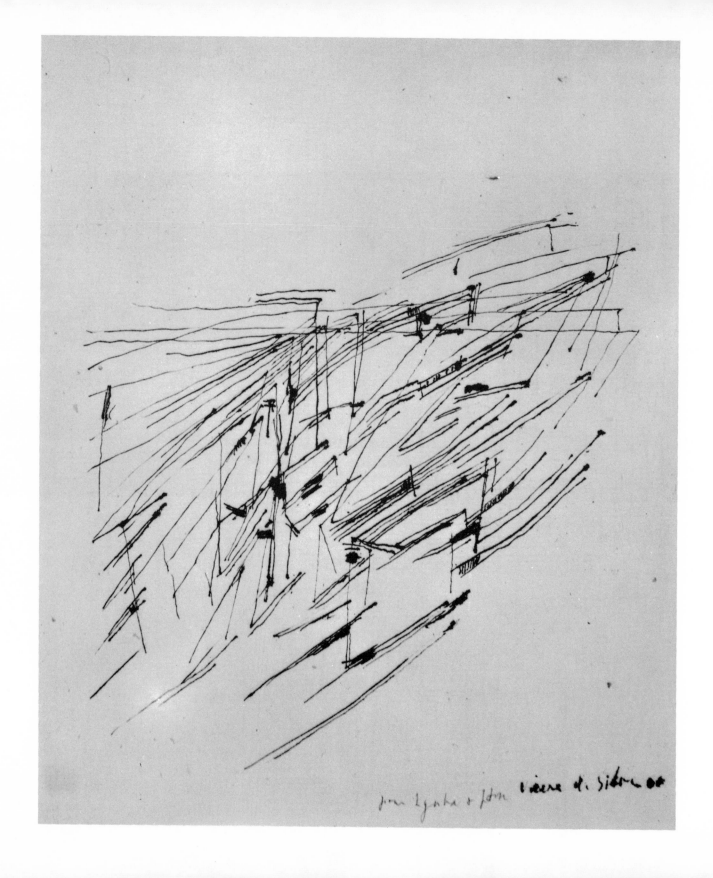

pour Lynda & John   viene di Sibiu 00

74

Plate 42
VIEIRA da Silva
Untitled Drawing, 1961
ink
11 ¾ x 9 ⁹⁄₁₆ inches (sight)
New York, Mr. and Mrs. John Lefebre

Plate 43
VIEIRA da Silva
Untitled Drawing, 1958
pastel
13 ⁵⁄₁₆ x 10 ⅜ inches (sight)
New York, Lefebre Gallery

Plate 44
Ernst Wilhelm NAY • *Untitled*, 1955 • water color, 16 x 23½ inches • New York, Joseph H. Hirshhorn Collection

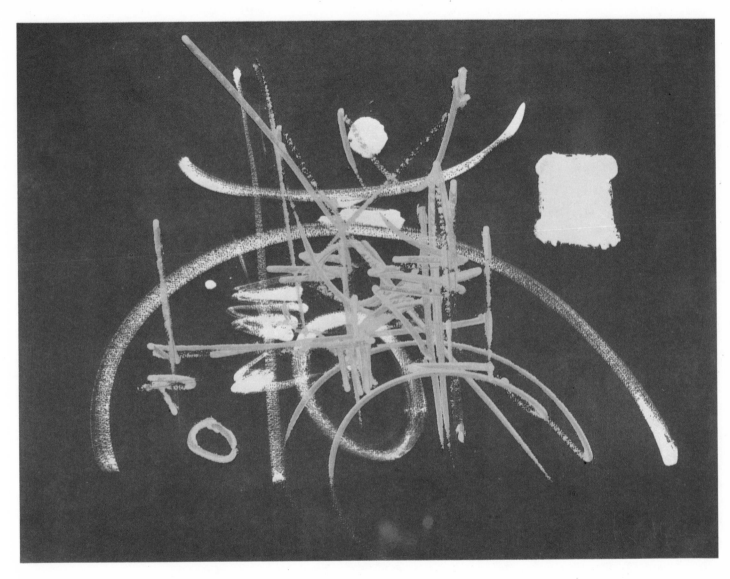

Plate 45
George MATHIEU · *Abstraction, 1956* · gouache, 24¾ x 19¼ inches · New York, Joseph H. Hirshhorn Collection

Plate 46
Giorgio MORANDI · *Still Life*, ca. 1958 · water color, 6 x 7¾ inches (sight) · New York, Mr. John Gordon

Plate 47
Walter MURCH
Study for "The Birthday," 1963
pencil, wash, crayon
23 x 17½ inches
New York, Collection of the Whitney Museum
of American Art
Neysa McMein Purchase Award

78

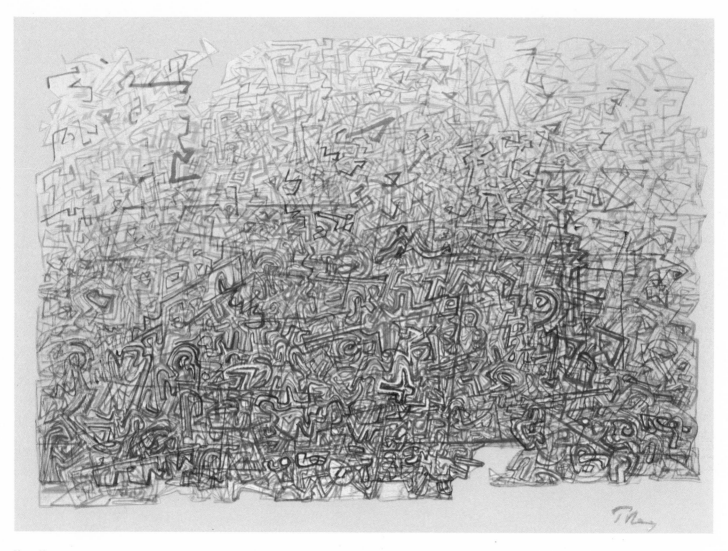

Plate 48

Mark TOBEY · *Announcement, 1950* · water color and gouache on cream paper, 18¾ x 24¾ inches
New York, Mr. Edgar Kaufmann, jr.

Plate 49

Arshile GORKY · *Study for painting, "They Will Take My Island,"* 1944 · pencil and wax crayon, 22 x 30 inches
New York, The Brooklyn Museum, The Dick S. Ramsay Fund

Plate 50
Jacques LIPSCHITZ
Rape of Europa, IV, 1941
gouache
26 x 20 inches
New York, Collection
The Museum of Modern Art
Gift of Philip L. Goodwin

Plate 51
Yasuo KUNIYOSHI
Girl Thinking, c. 1941
ink
9½ x 7 inches
New York,
Joseph H. Hirshhorn
Collection

Plate 52
Sam FRANCIS
Yellow into Black, 1958
water color on white paper
29¾ x 22 inches
Pittsburgh, Museum of Art,
Carnegie Institute

Plate 53
Adja YUNKERS
Tarassa X, 1958
pastel
44 x 31 inches
New York
Joseph H. Hirshhorn Collection

Plate 55
Leonard BASKIN · *Head of a Poet*, 1954 · brush and ink, 23½ x 29⅛ inches · New York, The Brooklyn Museum

Plate 54
José Luis CUEVAS
The Dwarf. Figure for a Crucifixion, 1956
pen and ink with wash
23½ x 19 inches
New York, The Brooklyn Museum

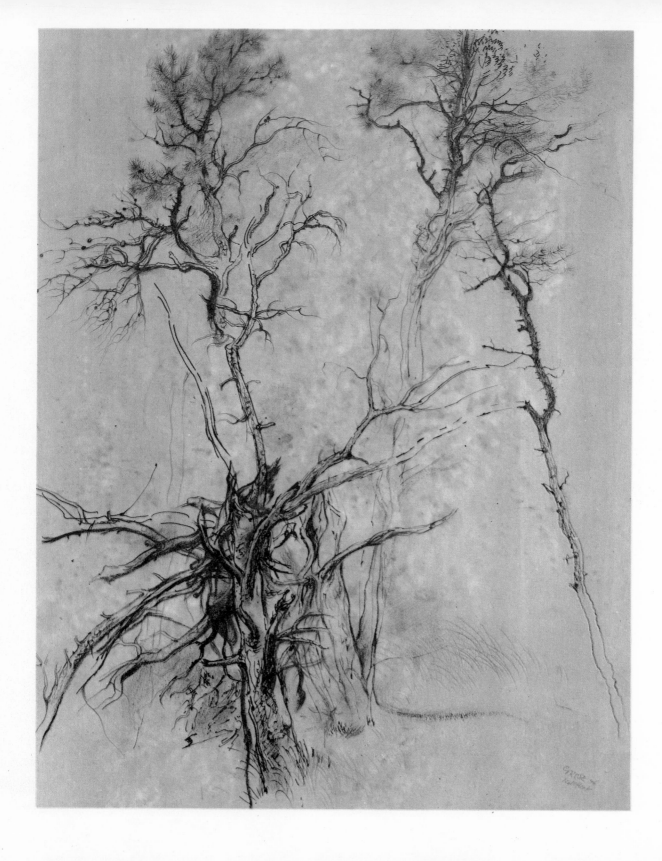

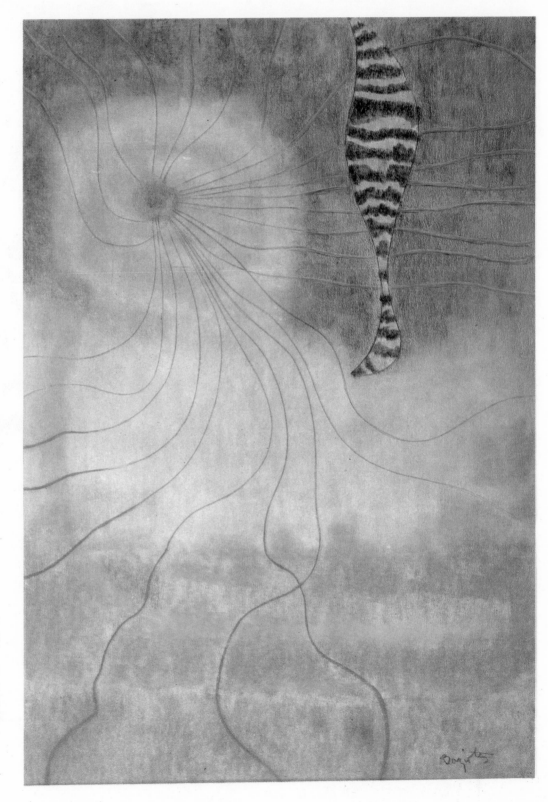

89

painting with two balls · 1960 j. johns

90

Plate 58
Jasper JOHNS
Painting with 2 Balls, 1960
pastel, charcoal and
pencil on paper
19½ x 15¼ inches
New York
Joseph H. Hirshhorn Collection

Plate 59
Julio GONZALES
Self Portrait, 1940
ink, pencil and brush
9½ x 6⅜ inches
Otterlo
Rijksmuseum Kröller-Müller

Plate 61
Hans HARTUNG • *Drawing in black, yellow and blue, 1960* • pastel, 19 x 28½ inches • New York, Lefebre Gallery.

Plate 60
Edouard PIGNON
Untitled Drawing, 1960
mixed media
14⅚ x 20 inches
New York, Mr. and Mrs. John Lefebre

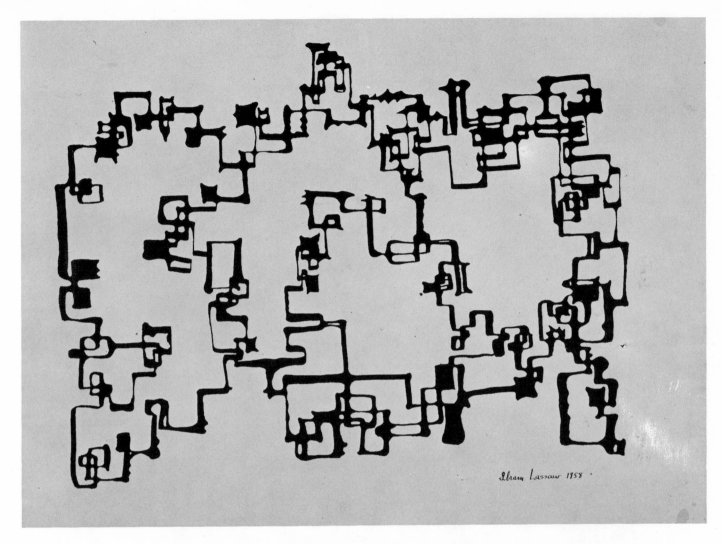

Plate 63
Ibram LASSAW · *Drawing for a Sculpture,* 1958 · brush and ink, 16½ x 22 inches · New York, The Brooklyn Museum
Gift of the Aaron E. Norman Fund, Inc.

Plate 62
Franz KLINE
Untitled, 1950 and reverse 1948
mixed media on paper
29½ x 22½ inches
New York, Mr. and Mrs. Robert C. Scull

95

Plate 64
Sam FRANCIS
Untitled, c. 1957
water color
24 x 19½ inches
New York
Joseph H. Hirshhorn Collection

Plate 65
Worden DAY
Magnetic Tide, 1961
ink and collage
36 x 16⅛ inches
New York, The Brooklyn Museum

97

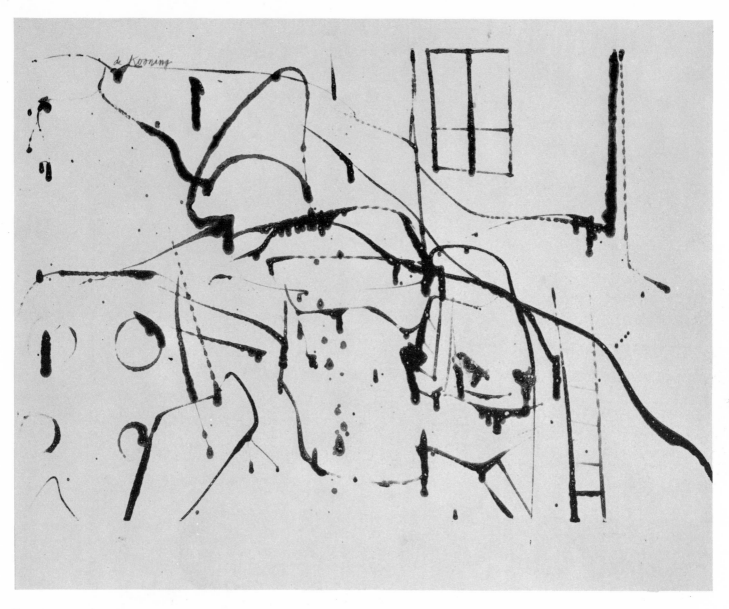

Plate 66
Willem de KOONING • *Composition, Attic Series*, 1950-51 • ink drawing, 29 x 35 inches • New York, Courtesy Sidney Janis Gallery

Plate 67
Bernhard LUGINBUHL
Title A, Study for Sculpture, 1961
pen, brush and ink
15¾ x 15½ inches
New York, The Brooklyn Museum

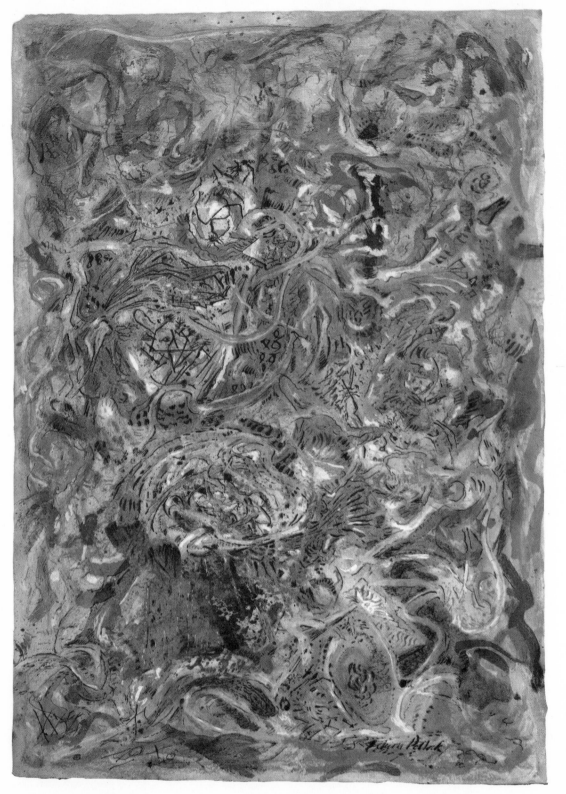

Plate 68
Jackson POLLOCK
Untitled, n. d.
water color and gouache
22½ x 15½ inches
New York
Joseph H. Hirshhorn Collection

Plate 69
Max WEBER
Contemplation, 1946-47
pastel
17¾ x 13 inches
New York
Joseph H. Hirshhorn Collection

Plate 70
Luis QUINTANILLA
Portrait Study of a Woman
1949
pencil
24⅛ x 16¾ inches
New York
The Brooklyn Museum

Plate 71
Alberto GIACOMETTI
Head of Boy, 1955
pencil
19½ x 12¾ inches
New York, Courtesy
Sidney Janis Gallery

Plate 73
Robert RAUSCHENBERG · *Mona Lisa*, 1960 · drawing and rubbing on paper, 22¾ x 28¾ inches
New York, Mr. and Mrs. Robert C. Scull

Plate 72
Robert RAUSCHENBERG
Portrait of Ethel Scull, 1962
combine drawing on white paper, four panels
58 x 46 inches
New York, Mr. and Mrs. Robert C. Scull

106

Plate 74
Calvin ALBERT
Ritual No. II, 1954
charcoal
29 x 23⅛ inches
New York, The Brooklyn Museum

Plate 75
Jean DUBUFFET
Site à la Rose, 1960
ink drawing
18 x 10¾ inches
New York
Courtesy Sidney Janis Gallery

Plate 76
Reginald BUTLER · *Circe Head*, 1951 · pencil, chalk, and wash on white paper, 10⅜ x 14⅜ inches
Ottawa, The National Gallery of Canada

Plate 77
Giacomo MANZU
Praying Cardinal, 1955
gouache
40¼ x 26½ inches
New York, Joseph H. Hirshhorn Collection

Plate 78

Pierre ALECHINSKY • *Drawing, 1956* • ink, 13⅛ x 16⅝ inches • New York, The Solomon R. Guggenheim Museum Collection

Plate 79

Mark TOBEY · *Remote Field*, 1944 · tempera, pencil and crayon, 28⅛ x 30⅛ inches · New York, Collection, Museum of Modern Art, Gift of Mr. and Mrs. Jan de Graaff

Plate 80

Marcel DUCHAMP • *Jacquette (Front and Back)*, 1956 • collage drawing, 16 x 23 inches • New York, Courtesy Sidney Janis Gallery

Plate 81
Claes OLDENBURG
Plan for Vacuum Cleaner from Side, 1964
chalk and wash
40 x 26 inches
New York, Courtesy Sidney Janis Gallery

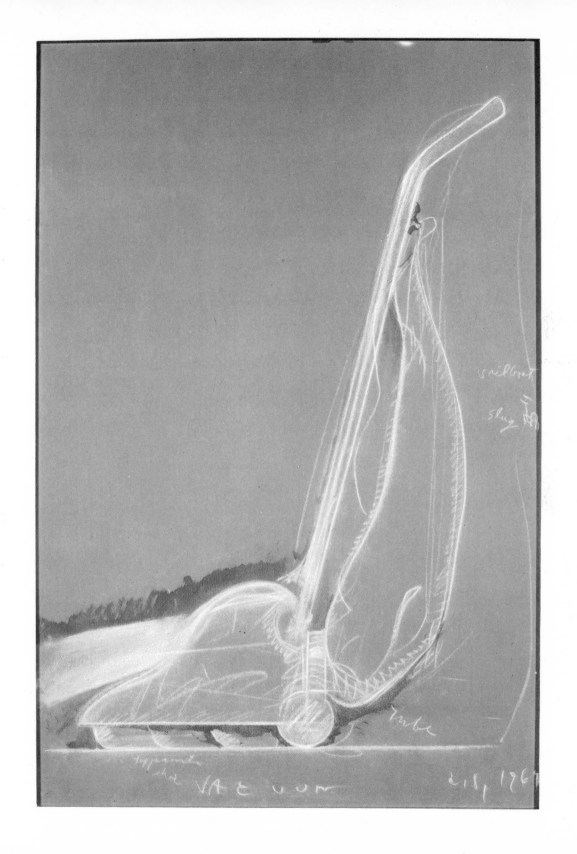

Plate 83
John Paul JONES • *Head*, 1960 • charcoal and pastel, 22¼ x 28 inches • New York, Collection, The Museum of Modern Art
Mr. and Mrs. Donald B. Straus Fund

Plate 82
Jean DUBUFFET
Black Countryside (Terres Noires), 1955
collage of painted paper
25½ x 23⅛ inches
New York, Collection, The Museum of Modern
Art, Gift of Mr. and Mrs. Donald H. Peters

Plate 84
Stuart DAVIS • *Underpass No. 1*, 1955 • gouache on paper, 9⅞ x 12⅝ inches • New York, Mr. and Mrs. Albert Dorne

Plate 85
Ben SHAHN
Studies of a Child, n.d.
brown pen and ink on yellowish paper
15¾ x 11¾ inches
The Artist's Collection

117

Plate 86

Lyonel FEININGER · *Church on the Cliff*, 1953 · charcoal, wash, pen and ink, 12⅞ x 19¼ inches · New York, Collection, The Museum of Modern Art, Gift of Mr. and Mrs. Walter Bareiss

Plate 87

Henry MOORE • *Woman Winding Wool*, 1949 • crayon and water color, 13¾ x 25 inches • New York, Collection, The Museum of Modern Art, Gift of Mr. and Mrs. John A. Pope in honor of Paul J. Sachs

Plate 88
Gabor PETERDI
Thorns, 1954
brush and ink
30¼ x 22¾ inches
Rowayton, Connecticut
Gabor Peterdi

Plate 89
Rico LEBRUN
The Furious Streetwalker
chased him out of the room
(illustration for Brecht's
"Threepenny Novel"), 1962
ink
26½ x 18½ inches (sight)
New York, Mrs. Ella Jaffe

The furious streetwalker
chased him out of the room.
Brecht, 3 penny Novel.

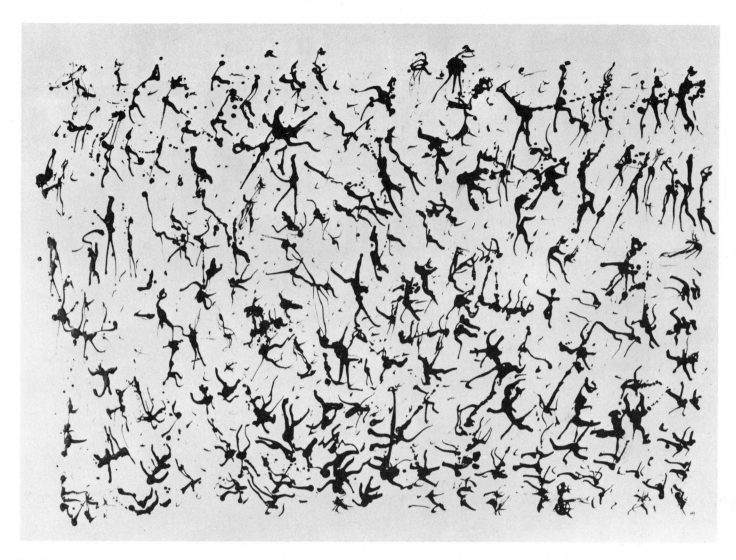

Plate 91

Henri MICHAUX • *Untitled*, 1960, dated on reverse • brush and ink, 29⅜ x 42½ inches • New York, Collection, The Museum of Modern Art, Gift of Michel Warren and Daniel Cordier

Plate 90

Joan MIRO

The Beautiful Bird Revealing the Unknown to a Pair of Lovers, 1941

gouache

18 x 15 inches • New York, Collection, The Museum of Modern Art

Acquired through the Lillie P. Bliss Bequest

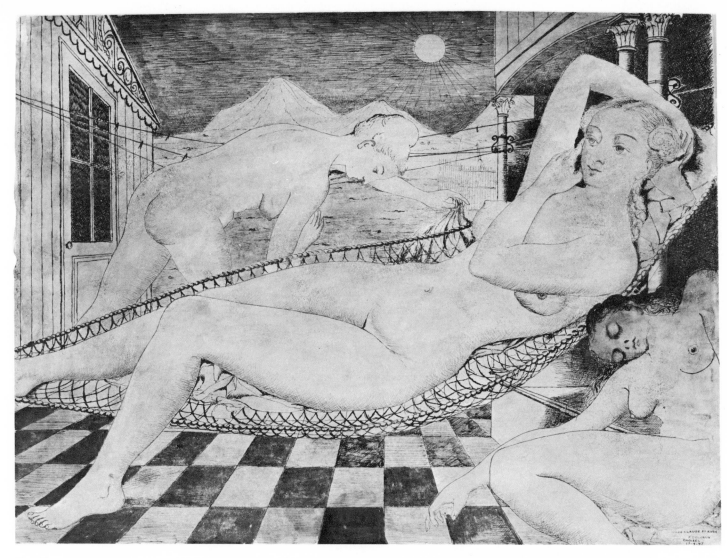

Plate 93
Paul DELVAUX • *At Claude and Ruth's, 1947* • wash, and pen and ink, 23½ x 30⅞ inches • New York, Collection, The Museum of Modern Art, The Kay Sage Tanguy Bequest

Plate 92
Eduardo PAOLOZZI
Drawing for a Saint Sebastian, 1957
ink, gouache and collage
13½ x 9⅞ inches
New York, The Solomon R. Guggenheim
Museum Collection

Plate 94
Henri MATISSE
Dahlias and Pomegranates
1947
brush and ink
30⅛ x 22¼ inches
New York, Collection
The Museum of Modern Art
Abby Aldrich Rockefeller
Fund

Plate 95
Fernand LEGER
Face and Hands, 1952
brush and ink
26 x 19¾ inches
New York, Collection
The Museum of Modern Art
Mrs. Wendell T. Bush Fund

Plate 96
Renato GUTTUSO
Head of a Girl, 1961
India ink and water color
18½ x 13⅜ inches
Milan, Collection Bolchini

Biographies

ALBERT
Calvin Albert (b. 1918) is an American sculptor and draughtsman who works mainly in metal and in the abstract idiom.

ALECHINSKY
Pierre Alechinsky (b. 1927) was born in Brussels and is a member of COBRA.

APPEL
Karel Appel (b. 1921) is a painter and sculptor who was born in Amsterdam. A co-founder of COBRA in 1949, he now lives in Paris. He is an exponent of Dutch Neo-Expressionism and Art Brut and has probably been influenced by Dubuffet.

BALTHUS
Balthus Klossowski de Rola (b. 1908) was born in Paris and now lives in Rome. His paintings have been influenced by the School of Paris.

BASKIN
Leonard Baskin (b. 1922) was born in New Brunswick, N. J., and studied art at Yale, the New School and in Paris. He now teaches at Smith College in Northampton, Mass.

BAZIOTES
William Baziotes (b. 1912) was born in Pittsburgh and is numbered among the more important Abstract Expressionist painters.

BECKMANN
Max Beckmann (1884-1950) was one of the German Expressionists. The subjects of his etchings and paintings were taken from everyday life: the city, the circus and fairs—used as symbols hinting at contemporary dangers. His major works were seven triptychs interpreting mythological themes and drawing comparisons between real life and the stage.

BISSIER
Julius Heinrich Bissier (b. 1893) is a German painter whose works show the influence of the teachings of Paul Klee.

BONTECOU
Lee Bontecou (b. 1931) is one of the young American women sculptors in the abstract vein working in New York.

BUTLER Reginald Butler (b. 1913) is an English sculptor whose welded steel figures seem inspired by the insect kingdom and the world of science fiction.

CALDER Alexander Calder (b. 1898), an American sculptor, was originally an engineer. He invented Stabiles and Mobiles, which can be regarded as a marriage between engineering and sculpture.

CORNEILLE Cornelis Van Beverloo, called Corneille, (b. 1922) was born in Belgium of Dutch parentage. He studied drawing in Amsterdam, but he is a self-taught painter. With Appel and Constant, he founded the experimental group, Reflex, and was one of the co-founders of COBRA. In his own work he is more poetic than his associates and shows influences of Klee and Miró.

CUEVAS José Luis Cuevas (b. 1933) is one of the more progressive painters of Mexico in style although he works in the traditional subject matter of modern Mexican painting.

DAVIS Stuart Davis (1894-1964) was born in Philadelphia and moved to New York at an early age. He studied painting originally with Robert Henri. Retaining his own personal style throughout a revolutionary period in art, he was always the painter. His experiments in collage and the use of lettering were imitations of the textures, freeing him of the limitations that collage's use of man-made objects place on scale. His landscapes developed from "multiple views" to "single focus" in which he united the flat plane of the working surface.

DAY Worden Day (b. 1916) is an American woman painter working in the abstract vein.

DELVAUX Paul Delvaux (b. 1897) was born in Belgium and teaches at the academy in Brussels. Originally he was a landscape painter but in 1935, during a trip to Italy, he discovered de Chirico's metaphysical painting and Surrealism.

DUBUFFET Jean Dubuffet (b. 1901) was born in France. His belated career as an artist began in 1942 when he became a painter and lithographer. Specializing in assemblages and experimentation with materials previously not used in painting, he is an exponent of Art Brut.

DUCHAMP   Marcel Duchamp (b. 1887), a French painter, was one of the original Dadaists. Before the invention of Dada, he had shocked New York with his *Nude Descending a Staircase* in the Armory Show of 1913.

ERNST   Max Ernst (b. 1881), a German artist who now lives in Paris, introduced the Dada movement into Cologne in 1919. He makes collages and frottages, and, since 1924, he has been associated with Surrealism.

FEININGER   Lyonel Feininger (1871-1956) was originally a caricaturist. Later the American Feininger came into contact with the Cubists, Delaunay and Der Blaue Reiter group. He transformed Cubism in a poetic and romantic way in paintings of seemingly-transparent rainbow hues. In 1919 he joined the Bauhaus and kept up the association until its dissolution in 1933. After his return to America in 1937, his sensitive atmospheric painting—formerly of old German towns—began to feature New York skyscrapers.

FRANCIS   Sam Francis (b. 1923) was born in California. During his recovery in a service hospital from wounds incurred in World War II, he became interested in painting. Since 1947 he has been a *tachiste* and moved to Paris in 1950 where he lives.

GIACOMETTI   Alberto Giacometti (b. 1901), a Swiss sculptor was born in Stampa to a Swiss painter. After studying art in Geneva and Rome, he moved to Paris where he has had his studio ever since. Until 1928, his figures resembled primitive sculptures and Cubist theories, but later his elongated bronze figures have more in common with Surrealism.

GONZALES   Julio Gonzales (1876-1942) was born in Barcelona but arrived in Paris in 1900 where he remained. Until 1927, he was a painter and an early associate of Picasso. Not widely known or appreciated during his lifetime, his metal repoussé figures have exerted a great influence on younger sculptors in Europe and America since his death.

GORKY   Arshile Gorky (1904-1948) was an Armenian who came to the United States and whose paintings have had a great deal of influence on younger artists working today. Originally his work was strongly inspired by Picasso.

GRAVES Morris Graves (b. 1910) is an American painter who has traveled in Japan, France and Mexico where he studied art collections. His works are in the tradition of American romantic painting, tinged with Oriental mysticism.

GROSZ George Grosz (1893-1959) was a German caricaturist and, after World War I, produced lithographs exposing post-war conditions with biting sarcasm. In them he attacked militarism, philistinism, and bureaucracy and capitalism with equal venom. After coming to New York in 1933, he turned to water colors of the city and rather Baroque still life. During World War II he painted symbolic, terror-filled anti-war pictures which rank as the most powerful of the kind.

GUSTON Philip Guston (b. 1913) was born in Montreal and lives in New York and is one of the influential American painters of Abstract Expressionism.

GUTTUSO Renato Guttuso (b. 1912) is a painter and influential teacher who was born in Sicily and now lives in Rome.

HARTUNG Hans Hartung (b. 1904) was a German painter, influenced by Kokoschka, Nolde and Marc who traveled to Paris in 1925 and 1930. In 1935 he left Germany ahead of the gestapo and fled to Paris where he was naturalized in 1946 and now works as an abstract painter.

HOFMANN Hans Hofmann (b. 1880) was born in Germany but, since the Nazi persecution of artists, has lived in the United States where he has exerted an enormous influence on the younger artists of the last two decades. He formed his new style of abstract, dynamic and colorful paintings from 1940 to 1944 and has inspired much of the work of Abstract Expressionists.

JOHNS Jasper Johns (b. 1930) is an American painter who is important for his creation of radically new forms of representation and is closely associated with Pop Art.

JONES John Paul Jones (b. 1924) was born in Iowa and studied in his own region at Iowa State University where he worked with Mauricio Lasansky and others, primarily in the graphic arts, in an abstract and romantic manner. He now teaches at U.C.L.A.

JORN Asger Jorn (b. 1914) was born in Denmark and moved to Paris in 1936 where he studied in Léger's atelier and collaborated with LeCorbusier. A painter, sculptor, engraver and ceramist, he has spent a long time in Italy and now divides his time between Paris and Amsterdam. He was co-founder of COBRA.

KLINE Franz Kline (1911-1962) was one of the important members of the New York School of Abstract Expressionist painters.

de KOONING Willem de Kooning (b. 1904) was born in Rotterdam but now lives in New York. His black-and-white abstractions, first exhibited in 1948, established him as one of the most important leaders (along with Pollock) of the new American painting. He often makes hundreds of preparatory drawings for each painting.

KUBIN Alfred Kubin (1877-1959) was a German draughtsman, watercolorist and teacher.

KUNIYOSHI Yasuo Kuniyoshi (1890-1953) was a Japanese artist who made his career in the United States as an influential painter and teacher.

LASSAW Ibram Lassaw (b. 1913) was born in Alexandria, Egypt, to parents of Russian descent. He is a metal sculptor who now works in New York.

LEBRUN Rico Lebrun (1900-1964) came to the United States from Naples and lived and taught in California. His painting style was forceful and individual and, although influenced by abstractionism, always figural in treatment.

LÉGER Fernand Léger (1881 - 1955) was a French painter whose early block-like figures evolved, c. 1917, into a form of curvilinear Cubism based on the geometrical shapes of machinery with brilliant metallic surfaces. These forms also influenced his massive, robot-like figures and increased the effect of his clear grays and strong, unbroken colors.

LINDNER Richard Lindner (b. 1901) is a German painter who now lives in New York.

LIPCHITZ	Jacques Lipchitz (b. 1891) left his native Lithuania for Paris in 1909 where he was at first inspired by Cubism and was later associated with Juan Gris. During the Occupation, he fled to the United States where he now lives and works in Hastings-on-Hudson and exerts great influence on a number of young American sculptors.
LUGINBUHL	Bernhard Luginbühl (b. 1929) was born in Switzerland and is a sculptor who works mainly in metal.
MACIVER	Loren MacIver (b. 1909) is that rarity, a native New Yorker, whose work has absorbed some aspects of abstractionism without losing the essential romanticism of mood.
MANZU	Giacomo Manzu (b. 1908), an Italian sculptor, was initially influenced by Rodin and Degas. While primarily interested in character, his rendering of facial expressions often leads him to the point of caricature.
MARINI	Marino Marini (b. 1901) was born in Pistoia and studied sculpture in Florence and in Paris. Like most sculptors, he is one of the outstanding modern draughtsmen. Since 1940 he has been teaching at the Brera Academy in Milan and concentrating on the motif of horse and rider symbolizing homeless humanity.
MASSON	André Masson (b. 1896) is a French Surrealist painter. His later work is divided between the Expressionist and the calligraphic style. He makes frequent use of bird and plant motifs.
MATHIEU	Georges Mathieu (b. 1922) is a French avant-garde painter.
MATISSE	Henri Matisse (1869-1954) was a French sculptor and painter, the leading representative of Fauvism. Renouncing academic style, he developed instead along a Postimpressionistic line of brighter, simpler design and has influenced the development of 20th-century painting and design by his use of large surfaces of pure color, reducing aerial perspective to a minimum.

MATTA — Roberto Sebastian Matta Echaurren (b. 1912) is a Chilean painter, now living in Paris. Matta turned from Abstract Surrealism to compositions employing planes and orbits in such intricate relationships that each passage appears to be a special complication with its own contours and galaxies of "things" that expand infinitely.

MICHAUX — Henri Michaux (b. 1899) is a Belgian painter in the School of Paris greatly influenced by Oriental calligraphy since traveling in the Far East in 1933.

MIRÓ — Joan Miró (b. 1893) is a Spanish Surrealist painter who has worked mainly in Paris. In 1925 he took part in the First Surrealist Exhibition and, with Dali, was recognized as one of the leading Surrealists. His later work has become more abstract.

MONDRIAN — Piet Mondrian (1872-1944) was a Dutch painter who lived in Paris, London, and New York and was, together with Picasso, Klee and Kandinsky, one of the most influential artists in the development of present-day art. His form of abstractionism, called Neo-Plasticism, consisted principally of restricting forms to purely geometrical shapes, set at right angles to the horizontal or vertical axes and colored in the three primary colors and white, black or gray.

MOORE — Henry Moore (b. 1898), the English sculptor, in his early phase sought to bring back to sculpture the effect of square mass and "block rhythms" in a style whose forms were related to Egyptian and Pre-Columbian sculpture. He has worked in stone, wood and bronze with equal effect, sometimes piercing the material.

MORANDI — Giorgio Morandi (1890-1964) was born in Bologna. He became a member of the famous *Secessione* group in 1914. Shortly thereafter, he began his famous series of still-life studies which he never abandoned. He was always influenced by Cézanne. After a short period as a Futurist, he joined for a time the *pittura metafisica* group under de Chirico and Carlo Carrà. He has been considered the artist's artist because of the esteem in which his works are held by modern painters.

MOTHERWELL — Robert Motherwell (b. 1919) is a painter from the state of Washington who is an influential member of the New York School of action painters.

MURCH — Walter Murch (b. 1907) was born in Canada but is an American painter who manages to invest his realistic paintings of mechanical objects—valves, and the like—with an aura of romanticism.

NAY — Ernst Wilhelm Nay (b. 1902) is a German painter who represents the Abstract Expressionist school in Germany.

NOEL — Georges Noel (b. 1924) is an abstract painter who lives in Paris.

OLDENBURG — Claes Thure Oldenburg (b. 1929) was born in Stockholm and studied at Yale and the Art Institute of Chicago. He now lives and works in New York and is primarily associated with the Pop-Art manifestations, especially "Environments," has created a number of "Happenings" and is represented in many collections.

PAOLOZZI — Eduardo Paolozzi (b. 1924) was born in Edinburgh. He is an important British sculptor who, critic Herbert Read declares, has created a wholly new style in modern sculpture.

PASMORE — Victor Pasmore (b. 1908) is one of the advanced abstract artists in England who began his career under the influence of Impressionism, then Fauvism and finally Cubism and abstract art. He has done mural reliefs which are three-dimensional constructions and some ceramic murals. He has associated with Ben Nicholson and Barbara Hepworth.

PETERDI — Gabor Peterdi (b. 1915) came to the United States from his native Hungary in 1939. He paints abstract landscapes but is primarily a printmaker and the author of a book on graphic arts. He teaches at the Yale School of Design.

PICASSO — Pablo Picasso (b. 1881) is a Spanish painter who studied and lives in Paris. His early works (1909-06) were conventional and named for their dominant colors, "blue" and "rose." Influenced by Iberian sculpture, African Negro masks and the art of Cézanne, he turned to compositions of angular planes which developed into Cubism. After a subsequent neoclassical period, a powerful new phase climaxed with the mural *Guernica* in 1937. He continues to produce paintings, sculptures and pottery in many styles simultaneously.

PIGNON	Edouard Pignon (b. 1905) is a French painter in the School of Paris.
PIPER	John Piper (b. 1903) is an English painter of linear and semi-abstract subjects.
POLLOCK	Jackson Pollock (1912-1956) studied art in Los Angeles and in New York. From 1938 to 1942 he was in the Federal Art Project. In 1940, he arrived at abstractionism. A complete nonconformist in painting, he invented "drip". He is perhaps the single most important artist (along with de Kooning) in the development of Abstract Expressionism.
QUINTANILLA	Luis Quintanilla (b. 1895/1905) is a Spanish artist who studied architecture for a time in Spain and joined Juan Gris in Paris where he became a Cubist painter. He is an important draughtsman and illustrator and now lives in New York.
RAUSCHENBERG	Robert Rauschenberg (b. 1925) is an American painter who uses images of the popular culture freely in realistic and abstract works.
RIVERS	Larry Rivers (b. 1923) is an American painter who presents commonplace objects in a new realist idiom.
SCHRAG	Karl Schrag (b. 1912) was born in Germany (his mother was an American) and now lives in New York where he teaches at Cooper Union. Influenced by Van Gogh and the German Expressionists, he is primarily a landscape painter.
SHAHN	Ben Shahn (b. 1898) left Lithuania for the United States as a young child. Apprenticed to a lithographer, he worked for a time and then traveled and studied in Europe. He chooses scenes of life in contemporary America for his paintings and prints.
SMITH	David Smith (b. 1906) is one of the most important modern American sculptors. Working mainly in abstract modes, his works are chiefly large in scale.
SONDERBORG	K.R.H. Sonderborg (b. 1923) is a Belgian painter, a member of COBRA and a bridge between European and American Action Painting.

de STAËL   Nicolas de Staël (1914-1955) was born in St. Petersburg and died in France. Most of his life he was influenced by the currents of contemporary French painting.

SUTHERLAND   Graham Sutherland (b. 1903) was born in Kent, England, and became a painter at age thirty. From 1940 to 1943 he was an artist in the War Office. The thorn series of drawings was part of the preparation for his Crucifixion painting in the Northampton Church in 1946. In 1952 he designed the tapestry for the restored Coventry Cathedral. His study of nature is very close to Surrealism.

TANGUY   Yves-Tanguy (1900-1955) was a French painter in close touch with the currents of modern French art. During the Occupation, he came to the United States and helped interest young American painters in European art developments, especially Surrealism.

TING   Walasse Ting (b. 1929) left Hong Kong and went to Paris where he is a painter, printmaker and ceramist.

TOBEY   Mark Tobey (b. 1890) was born in Wisconsin and traveled in Europe and the Far East and now lives in Seattle. His invention in painting is the "white writing" which is based on the technique of Chinese calligraphy.

VIEIRA   Maria Elena Vieira da Silva (b. 1908) was born in Portugal but moved to Paris in 1927 where she has since become an important exponent of the style of the School of Paris. For a time she studied sculpture with Bourdelle and Despiau and engraving with Hayter and worked in the Studios of Othon Friesz and Léger. She also made cartoons for tapestries and illustrated books. During World War II, she went to South America, returning to Paris in 1947.

VILLON   Jacques Villon (1875-1963), whose real name was Gaston Duchamp, was the brother of Marcel Duchamp and the sculptor, Duchamp-Villon. He began as a Cubist and founded *Section d'Or,* the avant-garde group which was concerned above all with ideal proportions (the "golden mean" or "section"). His painting contained definite constructional elements. Never completely non-figurative, he reduced natural themes to a kaleidoscopic surface shapes, relying on color for spatial effects.

WEBER	Max Weber (1881-1961) was America's earliest pioneer in modernism. Asserting that he depended on "the great ancients of all races and climes" for inspiration and incentive, his early work evidenced his religious nature with themes of prayer and contemplation and pictures of women suggestive of biblical passages. His later work was characterized by a freely-distorted Naturalism.
WILDE	John Wilde (b. 1919) is an American painter whose works have been described as "immaculate realism."
WOLS	Alfred Otto Wolfgang Schultze, called Wols, (1913-1951) was born in Berlin but lived in exile in Paris during the war where he remained afterwards. Influenced by Klee, Kandinsky and other members of the Bauhaus, he experimented in psychic improvisations.
WYETH	Andrew Wyeth (b. 1917) is an American painter in the romantic tradition whose individual style contains a form of symbolism and nostalgia presented by a meticulous technique.
YUNKERS	Adja Yunkers (b. 1900) was born in Latvia and came to America in 1947 where he is now associated with the painters called the New York School.

Bibliography

GENERAL

Barr, A. H., Jr., *Masters of Modern Art,* New York, 1954.

Brion, M., *L'Art Abstrait,* Paris, 1956.

Bru, C. P., *Esthétique de l'Abstraction,* 1955.

Canaday, John, *Mainstreams of Modern Art: David to Picasso,* New York, 1962.

Carrieri, R., *Il Disegno Italiano Contemporaneo,* Milan, 1945.

Cassou, J., and Jaccottet, P., *Le Dessin français au XXe siècle,* Lausanne, 1951.

Fuchs, H., *Gaben des Augenblicks, Vierundvierzig unveröffentlichte Zeichnungen und Aquarelle aus der Sammlung E. Frey,* Munich, 1964.

Grohmann, W., *The Expressionists,* New York, 1962.

Kuhn, C., *German Expressionism and Abstract Art,* the Harvard Collections, Cambridge, Mass., 1957.

Rauh, E. and Simon, S., A Catalogue of *20th century Master Drawings,* New York, 1963, The Solomon R. Guggenheim Museum, New York, University Gallery, University of Minnesota, Minneapolis, The Fogg Art Museum, Harvard University, Cambridge.

Reynolds, G., *Twentieth Century Drawings,* London, 1946.

Rosenberg, J., *Great Draughtsmen from Pisanello to Picasso,* Cambridge, Mass., 1959.

Rosenblum, R., *Cubism & Twentieth-Century Art,* New York, 1962.

Sachs, P. J., *Modern Prints & Drawings,* New York, 1954.

Selz, P., *German Expressionist Painting,* Berkeley, Calif., 1957.

Seuphor, M., *L'Art Abstrait,* Paris, 1949.

Seuphor, M., *Abstract Painting: Fifty Years of Accomplishment, from Kandinsky to the Present,* New York, 1963.

Trier, E., *Zeichner des XX Jahrhunderts,* Berlin, 1956.

Valsecchi, M., *The Italian Moderns,* New York, 1962.

BASKIN

Worcester Art Museum, *Leonard Baskin: sculpture, drawings, woodcuts,* Worcester, Mass., 1956.

BECKMANN

Goepel, E., *Max Beckmann Der Zeichner,* Munich, 1962.

DAVIS

Goossen, E. C., *Stuart Davis,* New York, 1959.

DUBUFFET

Limbour, G., *L'art brut de Jean Dubuffet,* Paris, 1953.

ERNST

Waldberg, P., *Max Ernst,* Paris, 1958.

FEININGER

Hess, H., *Lyonel Feininger,* New York, 1962.

GIACOMETTI

Sylvester, D., *Alberto Giacometti: sculpture, paintings, drawings,* London, 1955.

GORKY

Schwabacher, E. K., *Arshile Gorky,* New York, 1947.

Seitz, W., *Arshile Gorky,* New York, 1962.

GROSZ

Grosz, G., *George Grosz Drawings,* New York, 1944.

MANZU

Argan, G. A., *Manzu: disegni,* Bergamo, 1948.

MATISSE

Barr, A. H., Jr., *Matisse: His Art and His Public,* New York, 1951.

Greenberg, C., *Matisse,* New York, 1962.

Humbert, A., *Henri Matisse, dessins,* Paris, 1956.

Seckel, C., *Henri Matisse,* Tübingen, 1956.

MIRÓ

Dupin, J., *Miró,* New York, 1963.
Hunter, S., *Joan Miró: His Graphic Work,* New York, 1962.

Soby, J. T., *Joan Miró,* New York, 1959.

MOORE

Read, H., *Henry Moore, Sculpture and Drawings,* London, 1955.

Valentin, C., *Henry Moore Sculpture and Drawings,* New York, 1944.

PASMORE

Marlborough New London Gallery, *Victor Pasmore,* London, 1964.

PICASSO

Arnheim, R., *Picasso's Guernica: The Genesis of a Painting,* Berkeley and Los Angeles, 1962.

Boeck, N., *Picasso,* New York, 1962.

Boudaille, G., *Picasso's Sketchbook,* New York, 1962.

Elgar, F., and Maillard, R., *Picasso,* New York, 1956.

Eluard, P., *Picasso Dessins,* Paris, 1952.

Geiser, B., *Picasso: Fifty-five Years of His Graphic Work,* New York, 1962.

Hunter, S., *Picasso (Cubism to the Present),* New York, 1962.

Jardot, M., *Pablo Picasso Drawings,* New York, 1959.

Sabartes, J., *Picasso Toreros,* New York, 1961.

POLLOCK

Robertson, B., *Jackson Pollock,* New York, 1960.

SHAHN

Soby, J. T., *Ben Shahn, His Graphic Art,* New York, 1957.

SUTHERLAND

Melville, R., *Graham Sutherland,* London, 1950.

TANGUY

Soby, J. T., *Yves Tanguy,* New York, 1955.

TOBEY

Seitz, W., *Mark Tobey,* New York, 1962.

VIEIRA DA SILVA

Knoedler Galleries, *Vieira da Silva,* Paris, 1963.